From Trials to Triumph

Life Built on Resilience and Love

Sally A Campbell

Published in United States of America
Publisher: Ebook Writing Experts

First Edition 2026
ISBN -

Prologue

Every life begins long before it can be explained. It begins in places, in voices, in routines that feel ordinary while they are happening but later reveal themselves as the foundations of character. My story did not start with certainty or achievement. It began with curiosity, resilience, and a quiet determination to keep moving forward even when direction was unclear.

I was shaped by land and labor, by silence and expectation. My earliest memories are rooted in a modest home and the steady rhythm of work that surrounded my family. There was no excess, but there was purpose. Effort mattered. Patience mattered. I learned early that stability is built, not given, and that progress comes from persistence rather than comfort.

From childhood, observation became a survival skill. I watched how adults carried responsibility, how disappointment was endured without spectacle, and how work continued regardless of circumstance. Illness interrupted my early years often enough to isolate me, yet those interruptions became unexpected teachers. When the body slowed, the mind learned to expand. Solitude sharpened curiosity and strengthened independence.

Education was never optional. It was an expectation grounded in discipline, not praise. I was encouraged to think, to question, and to work through difficulty rather than avoid it. Guidance was sometimes imperfect and pressure was often present, but the underlying message remained constant. Learning was an obligation to oneself.

My life did not follow a straight path. It moved through science, music, teaching, business, marriage, loss, and reinvention. Each transition demanded adjustment. Each setback forced a decision between retreat and adaptation. I rarely felt fearless, but I learned to be resolute. Forward motion became a habit long before it became a choice.

This book is not a record of ease or flawless progress. It is a reflection on persistence. It tells the story of building a life through effort, curiosity, and the willingness to change direction when necessary. It is about knowing when to endure and when to leave, when to accept guidance and when to trust one's own judgment.

With time, I came to understand that challenges are not detours. They are instruction. Failure refines judgment. Uncertainty demands growth.

This is not a story of triumph over others. It is a story of triumph over circumstance, doubt, and silence. What follows is how that life was shaped, tested, and ultimately claimed.

Dedication

This book is dedicated to my father and my second husband, Ken, both of whom are no longer here but remain deeply present in my thinking and work. They taught me how to understand the world through science, calculation, and experiment. More importantly, they helped me see reality as it is, not as I wished it to be, and gave me the tools to keep learning from it.

Acknowledgement

I would like to acknowledge Janet Hall, whose presence in my life over the past twenty years has been a steady source of encouragement, clarity, and support. Our relationship began in a formal setting, but over time it grew into a genuine and lasting friendship. In many ways, Janet has helped me keep going when I felt uncertain about what direction to take next, both in my work and in my personal life.

Janet has a rare ability to listen without judgment and to ask the kind of questions that quietly guide you toward your own answers. During moments when progress felt difficult or when circumstances seemed overwhelming, she helped me sort through problems, plan ahead, and regain the courage to move forward. Her encouragement was not loud or dramatic, but consistent, thoughtful, and deeply effective.

Writing this book required reflection, persistence, and a willingness to revisit experiences that were not always easy to examine. Throughout that process, Janet's steady support reminded me that forward movement does not require certainty, only commitment. She helped me trust that continuing the work, even in small steps, mattered.

I am also grateful for the many people who crossed my path over the years and contributed, knowingly or unknowingly, to the ideas and experiences that shaped this book. Teachers, colleagues, students, and friends all played a role in helping me observe the world more carefully and think more critically about my place within it.

Finally, I acknowledge the patience required to see a long project through to completion. This book represents not just a period of writing, but a lifetime of learning, questioning, and adapting. To those who supported me by simply believing that the work was worth doing, I offer my sincere thanks.

Table of Content

Chapter 1

Early Life in Wichita Kansas

My life began in Wichita, Kansas, on a stretch of land built on an acre and a half wide, yet large enough to hold my first home in this world. Wichita was known for its aircraft plants, railway construction and wide stretches of farmland. My earliest memories are rooted in that land, which I later learned had been a wedding present. My mother had purchased it and given it to my father when they got married. The gift was more than soil and grass. It was the foundation on which my earliest sense of home and family was built.

At the time of my birth, the land held a simple open-air cabin. My parents had worked hard to improve it before I arrived. They closed from the front, added a small room and built a bathroom and a kitchen. Those modest improvements became the setting for my first days of life. The cabin sat on a gentle hill and from there the land sloped down toward a larger five-acre. A railroad track cut across that space. The trains that roared past became a feature of my childhood. They carried the weight of industry and the promise of destinations beyond my reach.

That same land also became my playground. After rainfall, the lower ground flooded and turned into a miniature world of streams and ponds. I treasured wading through the water, following the tiny fish and building makeshift dams. Nature provided freedom that balanced the quiet rhythm of our household.

By the time I was three years older my parents had added another bedroom. I was given their first addition as my own room. Around the same time, they laid a brick patio in front of the cabin. My earliest lessons in craftsmanship came from helping to set those bricks in place. I could not have known then how useful the patience of that work would be.

Life inside the home was calm, sometimes even still. My mother devoted her time to sewing and knitting. She created order and comfort with her hands. My father lived a more complicated life. He had graduated from Harvard Law School because his own father needed a lawyer. My grandfather lost money through the Depression while advising others about investments. My father's training was about ambition and more about family responsibility.

Despite his education, my father never restricted his work to being a lawyer. He oversaw the estates that my grandfather had bought. One of them was an aluminum forge press which produced tank parts during the Second World War. I learned through him how America had an industry and politics bound together. He had been an active member of the Democratic Party and had been national vice president of the Young Democrats. Political discussions were common at our dinner table at home, although when I was too young, I could not understand the entire context.

My father tried to instruct me in mathematics and science, despite his long hours. But here my real interest came in a different variety. At the age of eight years, he presented me with his stamp collection. That gift has opened me to a world that I can hold in my hands. Those scraps of paper were narratives about countries, cultures and events way out of Kansas. Whenever he attempted to pull me back to lessons on physics or arithmetic, I would resist with the pretext that I had to play with the stamps. They made my hobby all the bigger in the world.

I was also ill in my childhood. Pneumonia came back again seven times. Every single time, the illness would put me out of school and my dad would not allow me to hold back out of my education. He did not accept excuses. It was his resolve that my education was not derailed even when my body failed.

My parents undertook another house expansion by the time

I was seven or eight years old. They included three bedrooms. Once the initial addition was done there was a crawl space below it. That gloomy, obscure place was the ideal location for my railroad model. In due course, and the two additional bedrooms were added, I could get the railroad to the attic. In the attic I had greater liberty and freedom. I became interested in trains- the real trains that rumbled by our country, and the little trains that I could run down their lines.

My parents had a swimming pool constructed when I was thirteen. It was almost an ambitious endeavor of a family with low income. Our neighbors inspired the idea to some degree. One of them had been a professional New York swimmer. She had relocated to Wichita to marry a man who operated a school of children with learning disabilities. Although she had a very busy life at home, she volunteered to teach us all how to swim in the neighborhood. I heard about her much earlier when we had no pool of our own.

I was excited to participate when my father finally decided to build one. I was with the carpenters and assisted in molding the wooden shapes into which the concrete was to be cast. On the day of the pour I sat on top of the frame and poured the mixture and watched it run into position. There was hard work but it was like a creating moment. It was not just recreation, but the pool. It was a teaching in the ability to transform the world around us through hard work, talent and vision.

Wichita itself was community and plenty of industries were there at the time. The Boeing plant was there and trains bore the signs of economy all over the place. My political activities by my father, the success of my grandfather in business and the industrial environment provided me with a premature feeling of potential. They recommended that there might be more to life than the one and a half acres that I was born to. Meanwhile, I was basing myself on the difference between our small five-room house and the thirteen-room house that my grandfather had in Tulsa. He was a vice president of the Kerr Glass and we visited him as glimpses of which I still recollect.

When I was older, I spent many days with him. He talked about work as though it was an obligation and a right. He demonstrated to me that money could also bring comfort, but it was discipline that brought respect. His universe was made of smooth wood, large objects and grandeur. Hammers, wet earth after a storm and the constant beat of trains filled the house. I was marked by both memories.

The greatest thing of those early years was no lesson on money or property. It was concerning hard work and effort. I was taught that life demanded constant planning, action and not giving up in the face of failure. My mother demonstrated to me how devotion might be silent and persevering. My father demonstrated to me an obligation that might require more than passion. My grandfather demonstrated to me prosperity had its own burdens. And the ground itself demonstrated to me that play, exploration and imagination might not be incompatible with struggle.

Now I see that it was not my home that I was given when I looked back at Wichita. It provided me with a resiliency base. I can still recall that Wichita provided me with the beat of industry and tranquility of nature. It taught me the earliest lessons in construction, of bricks, railroads, or concrete. It also provided me with the room to dream of the bigger world and it taught me to respect those who are beneath my feet. Those lessons influenced all the things that followed in my life.

Chapter 2

Father's Wisdom and Grandfather's Voice

The rhythm of my childhood was shaped by two men whose lives pulled me in different directions: my father and my grandfather. My father's voice was filled with restless ambition; dreams he had never fulfilled. My grandfather's was measured and steady, grounded in the discipline of daily work. Together, their guidance wove a tapestry of lessons that I still carry. One urged me to reach higher, the other reminded me to stand firm.

My father was a man of sharp intellect, a Harvard Law School graduate who carried the weight of choices made before him. He had dreamed of becoming a physicist, unraveling the mysteries of the universe, but the Great Depression and my grandfather's financial struggles sent him into law school instead. When I was born, he placed his deferred hopes on me, determined that I might live the life he could not.

Some of my earliest memories are when my father sitting at the kitchen table with **Scientific American** spread open like a map. He would point to diagrams of planets or atoms, explaining gravity or the motion of the stars with a spark in his voice. I was far too young to understand, perhaps only six years older, but his enthusiasm was contagious. Even when I resisted, his belief that I could achieve something great planted a quiet seed in me.

Science didn't stay contained to the pages of magazines. By the time I was in seventh grade, my father had transformed my old bedroom into a laboratory, a small sanctuary of discovery. A Bunsen burner flickered on the wooden table, its blue flame casting long shadows across the walls. A heavy microscope waited to reveal the organisms in the world which were too small for the naked eye. Shelves lined with beakers and test tubes caught the light, turning ordinary glass into something almost magical. My father showed me how to mix solutions and focus the lens, his hands steady while his voice hurried me along, urging me to notice every detail.

In high school, my father pushed the idea further. He organized a Saturday night science club and invited neighborhood boys to join. I hoped it would bring friendship, but instead it brought teasing. The boys laughed, chasing me back to my room and declaring that science wasn't for girls. Their words stung, but I refused to let them silence me.

Not every lesson landed the way my father intended. The science club fizzled under the weight of their jeers and I often resisted his relentless push toward physics. At those times I preferred the quiet focus of my stamp collection or the freedom of exploring the valley behind our house. Yet even in resistance, I learned something valuable: the strength to keep going, even when others doubted me.

My father's lessons extended beyond the lab. He ran a hardware store in Wichita, a place alive with the clang of metal and the sharp smell of paint. After World War II, he also managed a steel forge press that produced the tank underbodies and later oversaw a motel in Kansas City. These ventures, passed down from my grandfather, demanded long hours and constant energy.

By 1946, when I was about five years older, I remember my father coming home from the store each night, emptying his pockets and spreading the day's earnings on the living room floor. The coins glinted under the lamp as he stacked them into neat piles, explaining how each sale added up. I watched with wide eyes, as if the small towers of nickels and dimes were treasures, each one proof of his effort.

As a teenager, I worked alongside with my father in the store. I sold tools, stocked shelves and even helped build air conditioners;

the kind that cooled Kansas homes with water trickling through fiber nets. The hum of the fans, the smell of sawdust and the weight of a wrench in my hand felt like a bridge into his world. Those summers taught me that business wasn't only about money. It was about solving problems for people, one sale at a time.

While my father urged me toward science and commerce, my grandfather anchored me in the value of steady work. Before moving to Wichita, he had taught business to me in Oklahoma and later he opened the first national savings bank. His life was a testament to resilience; when the stock market crashed and his clients lost money on his advice, he repaid them from his own pocket. By the time I was in ninth grade, he had built a new home just a few blocks from ours, a place filled with polished wood, quiet mornings and the quiet authority of discipline.

Most mornings, I ride my bicycle there at five o'clock, the streets are still dark and cool. He was always awake, dressed and ready to begin his day. My grandmother, who was a Southerner by habit, woke up just as early as she was. She would hand me a cup of strong, bitter coffee and I would sit with my grandfather for an hour while he spoke about buying and selling properties. His voice was steady, unhurried and full of certainty.

My grandfather did not have any great tales about his life or addresses about success. Rather, he would tell me the practical facts of the deals he was doing, to remind me that life was not constructed in abstractions. It was constructed in the daily toil. Such mornings were a ritual for me. Then my grandmother would make breakfast.

The aroma of the cooked bacon was so strong in the house and my dad came to drive me to school. Three to four years of such routine made me. I might not have walked away with certain guidelines in my mind, but the message was clear: to live well, a person needed to continue moving, continue working and continue building.

They never slept and neither were they supposed to expect me to. I was not burdened by that expectation. It was a silent assumption that I could create something myself.

When I started high school, my parents had a small playhouse placed behind my new bedroom. It was constructed many years ago on my behalf and on behalf of my friends but it became my refuge by that time. I had a study and experimenting space in its wooden walls. It was there that I made the preparations on the projects which would one day take me to the National Science Fair.

My dad did not often personally direct those efforts; days were taken up with the store. But his unchanging confidence in his silent insistence upon the fact that I could do more, which led me to try. In retrospect, I now realize how I was influenced by my father and grandfather in various aspects. The magazines and laboratory work of my father had created a seed of interest that helped me to endure the hardships though I may never become the physicist just like my father had imagined me to be.

Working early in the morning is the way that my grandfather used to wake up and in contrast, taught me that work was not only a responsibility but something that I always had to make the world around me. They left me between them without any easy answers, but with questions to be pursued and the belief that perseverance was its own form of wisdom.

Chapter 3

Curious Mind in Silent House

My childhood house was full of hours of silence and expansive areas and I was taught at a young age how to fill that silence with my own escapades. When I was eight years old, I usually walked around the creek that was behind our house or sat before the fire reading a book. Such lonely periods made me and made me depend upon curiosity and imagination as my constant companions.

And it was not always a haven in the house. The stinging words of my mother might send me to the hiding place where she cannot hear me behind the door in the closet. Even then I started to find strength in myself. The desire to resist, to make a way in a world that either seemed too big or too small.

Nevertheless, there was a beat in our house. Evenings would take a routine even when I was eight years old. I would come out of school at about six thirty o clock and in most cases, my mother took me to different activities. My father arrived home later, at about seven o clock, but in winter his arrival was signified by the constant heat of the fireplace. That fire, rustling with silence, made our house seem to be warm even when there was not much to say.

I used to sit on the floor by the fire, coloring in a book or working on little projects, the crackle of fires had me worried. Others dined out, and my mother put up with her sewing long enough to accompany us. On a few occasions, she used to prepare meals at home and then I would immerse myself in a jigsaw puzzle or a book till I went to sleep at eight in the night.

My father had retired early, and my mother kept up late, until two or three in the night, and sewing her quilt without any noise.

The evenings were somewhat of an unnatural equilibrium and there was loveliness in the house but not necessarily dialogue.

I was left to myself so frequently, that I became independent, a quality which became wild and uncontrollable, as the flowers of our valley. Having little expectation of me in the way of chores, I came to know how to fill my hours. I read, assembled bits of puzzles, or created little projects, each of which was a silent discovery that I could count on myself.

When our house was expanded, I moved my model railroad into the attic, arranging tracks that carried my imagination to faraway places. Before that, I had set it up in the cool basement, where the hum of the tiny engines echoed against stone walls. Sometimes a dog wandered through and I would pause to pet it before returning to my world of trains. Those hours alone taught me that solitude was not emptiness. It was a space where I could think, create and prove to myself that I could always find something worth doing.

Outside, the land itself became my playground. The creek behind our house was my favorite place, especially after heavy rain when it swelled into streams and shallow pools. I waded in barefoot, the water cold against my ankles, stacking stones to redirect the current just to see what might happen. It wasn't science, at least not yet it was pure play, the joy of shaping something that felt like my own. I chased the water's path through the valley, exploring what grew along its banks, always curious about where it might lead.

By sixth grade, my father had set up a high jump practice area in the yard. Each time I cleared the bar, a jolt of pride surged through me. The yard also bloomed with his daffodils so striking that he later became a national judge for them. I wandered among their bright yellow faces, marveling at the way they nodded in the Kansas wind, beauty standing firm in its season.

Summers carried me to the neighbors' improvised pool across

the stream, where me and other children's splashed and shouted until the light faded. Winters shifted us indoors, into their basement, where we practiced riflery on a range their father had built. The sharp crack of each shot echoed off the walls and they were both thrilling and unsettling. After school, baseball filled our evenings. Dust rose from the field as we ran the bases, until my mother's call for dinner pulled me back home.

Those quiet hours, indoors and out, built my sense of self. Whether I was piecing together a puzzle by the fire or stacking stones in the creek, I felt capable like I could find a way through anything. Even when pneumonia struck me, again and again before high school, I refused to let it hold me still. Seven times it kept me away from classmates, yet I filled the days with reading, drawing, or quiet experiments. Illness slowed my body, but it never stilled my mind.

My mother, though, brought challenges of another kind. When my father stayed late at the store, her frustration often spilled into sharp words. At those times, I sometimes slipped into a closet, curling up in the dark until her voice softened or faded. One memory stands out: I was five years old, crouched under a stone table in the courtyard after some misunderstanding with our dog. My mother stood over me, asking why I had hurt it. I don't remember what I had done if anything but I remember the weight of her voice, the way it froze me in place.

There were other moments too standing stiff as she pinned the hem of a dress she had sewn, fidgeting under her sharp corrections, or shrinking when she scolded me for a messy room. Those times made the house feel heavy, as though I were somehow in the way. When the walls pressed too close, I ran to the valley, where the air felt kinder and the creek offered freedom. Still, I never felt barred from exploring or building because I was a girl who was not until high school. When carpenters or painters worked on our home, I lingered nearby, looking closely and sometimes offering a hand. No one told me I couldn't.

Standing up for myself became a habit that grew stronger with time. Later, in college and beyond, I faced similar doubts, like the day I investigated air pollution at a hospital. The power plant workers questioned me, insisting that I did not look like an expert. I replied by asking whether they put nutmeg in their boilers. The remark caught them off guard and reminded me that I belonged, even in places where others doubted me.

My models for independence were close at hand. My father and grandfather, through their tiring work, showed me what it meant to keep moving forward. My grandmother carried her own quiet strength, tracing our family line back to the Mayflower while staying active in her community. Even a teacher in third or fourth grade left a mark on me, encouraging my questions, though her name has since faded from memory.

That teacher opened a door to deeper curiosity and the combination of those early influences with my freedom to explore prepared me for challenges ahead. By the time I reached adolescence, I was already learning how to handle conflict, whether it was my mother's temper or arguments with neighborhood children over a game of baseball. That skill only grew sharper and later helped me in graduate school at Johns Hopkins, where I had to resolve disputes and plan effectively. It became equally important when I ran my own business and managed a team that sometimes veered off track.

Independence, nurtured from childhood, taught me that life was about meeting challenges head-on. Whether in a creek, in a classroom, or in a boardroom, the lesson was the same.

Looking back, I see that the freedoms and struggles of my early years became the roots of my resilience. The quiet hours by the fire, the dams I built in the creek and the times I stood firm in the face of exclusion all shaped me into someone who could face the world with confidence. I learned to find my place, to keep moving forward and to trust that I would figure things out no matter what came next.

Chapter 4

Determination and Challenges

My struggles in childhood came in many forms. Vision problems, unnoticed until a humiliating moment in third grade, added one more obstacle. My mother often left me to fend for myself, forcing me to navigate daily life with little guidance. Yet in the stillness of those hardships, I discovered a resilience that became my foundation. Whether I was building experiments for the National Science Fair or diving into a pool to retrieve a lost watch, I learned to meet setbacks with quiet determination that would carry me forward.

Illness was an even earlier companion. Pneumonia shadowed my childhood, striking me seven times before I reached high school. Each bout left me confined to bed, the air heavy with the strain of breathing. My mother would call the pediatrician and he would spend what felt like endless minutes examining me, his calm voice deciding whether it was pneumonia again or only a stubborn cough.

Once, I was admitted to the hospital, the sharp antiseptic smell clinging to everything. My aunt visited, her face a small comfort in the blur of that stay. Illness steals from me: playdates with other children, afternoons of running outside and weeks of freedom each year. Yet even then, I searched for ways to stay occupied, refusing to let sickness erase my sense of movement and purpose.

Schooling was not as disrupted by my illnesses as one might expect. By the time I entered public school, the worst of the pneumonia bouts had passed. I kept pace with lessons, my mind sharp even when my body faltered. When sickness confined me indoors, I often sat by the window, restless and frustrated by the doctor's instructions to stay in bed. Those enforced pauses, though uncomfortable, taught me a kind of patience I would only come to understand later.

Another challenge crept in quietly: my eyesight. For years I sat in the front row, where the blackboard's chalk marks appeared clear enough. I assumed everyone else saw the world as I did, edges blurred but tolerable.

The truth came out in third grade. One morning I arrived late and was placed in a back seat. When the teacher asked me to read from the board, I squinted, but the words dissolved into blur. Mistaking my struggle for defiance, she sent me into the closet. The darkness wrapped around me, heavy with embarrassment. When I was finally let out, I confessed that I could not see the board. My mother was called, but it was my father who took me to the eye doctor. She seemed too afraid to face the truth.

My mother's neglect was a quieter kind of challenge, one that shaped me in ways I did not recognize until years later. By the time I reached second or third grade, I was largely on my own. She had cared for me as an infant, but by the time I was six years older and I cannot recall her feeding me or tending to my daily needs.

Even meals blur in my memory. I have no clear recollection of lunches at home. Sometimes I ate at school and once in a while she took me to a Mexican restaurant when I was older, but at home I do not remember opening the refrigerator or being served a plate of food. I must have been provided for somehow, yet the details are lost, as if her absence erased them.

Her distance forced me to solve problems early. By sixth grade, I was managing my days without her guidance. That self-reliance became my armor, the way I learned to move through a house where love existed but was rarely expressed in words or care.

Those struggles set me apart from my peers, though I did not dwell on it at the time. My days, shaped by illness and solitude, gave me a rhythm of my own. While other children played after school, I was often in my backyard playhouse or tucked away in my room with a book. I did not compare myself to them. I simply kept moving forward, finding my own way.

Confidence came in small, steady steps. In sixth grade, my father built a high jump setup in the yard and each time I cleared the bar, I felt a rush of strength. Playing football with a neighbor boy, helping him practice for the high school team, gave me the thrill of being useful.

Grades offered another kind of encouragement. Teachers praised me on my report cards, their words a quiet validation. My father would sometimes pose a problem for me to solve and finding the answer felt like victory. These small triumphs built in me a certainty that I could handle what came my way.

Support came mostly from within the family. My teachers were kind, but I do not recall neighbors or friends stepping in when I needed encouragement. My grandparents, however, provided warmth and steadiness, especially when my mother's attention faltered. Their quiet faith in me was enough to keep me going.

My future began to take shape in the projects I undertook alone, especially in science. At dawn I slipped into my backyard playhouse, driven only by curiosity. One year I studied mold on a tobacco plant, setting up experiments, adjusting conditions and recording the results. That project won at the local science fair and carried me to the National Science Fair. The next year I investigated surface tension in water, designing equipment to measure it and once again succeeded.

My parents did not even know what I was working on until they were asked to drive me to the fair. Those projects were more than experiments. They were proof that I could create something out of nothing, that independence and persistence could take me further than anyone expected.

Resilience revealed itself in fleeting moments. I remember diving to the bottom of a pool to retrieve a dropped watch, the cold and heavy water around me. I do not recall every detail, only the determination that pushed me through challenges, whether it was fixing something stubborn or facing a task that tested my grit. Illness taught me persistence too, especially as I grew older and learned to rest when a cough lingered.

There was also the moment at age five when I stepped into a pot of boiling water my mother had left beside my bed. The burn sent me to the hospital and through countless doctor visits. The pain and her carelessness left a scar deeper than the one on my skin. It sharpened my instinct to care for myself, to be watchful in ways a child should not have needed to be.

Creative outlets became my refuge. Beyond science fairs, I found comfort in Campfire Girls, where I crafted pictures and projects with my hands always busy. In the sandbox I built bridges and buildings, testing their strength and imagining how to improve them. At the creek I stacked stones to redirect the current, creating dams that shifted the flow. Each act of making, whether with sand, wood, or water, kept my mind engaged and gave me a sense of control through the hardest years.

Looking back, I see that those struggles became the crucible of who I am. From my earliest years I have been solving problems and working around obstacles, whether it was pneumonia, a blurry blackboard, or my mother's absence. That instinct carried me into college and eventually into my own business. It felt like a natural step for someone raised among entrepreneurs, with a grandfather who was vice president of Kerr Glass and parents whose lives were steeped in responsibility. Business was not only survival. It was proof that I could face any challenge and find a way through.

If I could speak to my younger self, I would tell her that she was already finding her way. I would tell her to keep moving forward and to trust that every problem holds a solution, even if it takes time to see it. Those early hardships, from illness to neglect, did not break me. They built me. They taught me to stand alone, to persist and to believe in the quiet strength that was already growing inside me.

Chapter 5

Singing in Choirs & Learning Through Campfires

In the quiet corners of my childhood, I found joy in the harmony of a choir and the steady glow of a campfire. Those moments, filled with song and shared projects which gave me a sense of belonging that balanced the solitude of my days. My father's short-lived science clubs, though disfigured by teasing boys, planted seeds of curiosity that grew into a lifelong love of discovery.

Campfire Girls offered a refuge, a place to build skills and friendships away from the tensions at home. Through it all, I faced doubts about my place as a girl in a world of science, but each challenge sharpened my resolve, teaching me to keep at it, to find my voice in both music and knowledge.

Responsibilities have never been a heavy burden in our house, but when they came, I moved through them with a quiet mantra be patient, this will be over. I'd sweep or tidy, whispering to myself to keep going. A lesson my parents instilled from the time when I was young.

Singing didn't weave into those tasks; it was a soft habit that started when I was four years older. Music wasn't a lifeline for me but also it was not like it might be for others. It was just something I did; a pleasant distraction. Piano lessons, pushed by my parents, were more effort than joy, my fingers stumbling over keys as I worked to master them. Singing, though, was lighter, a spare-time pleasure that didn't ease life's struggles; didn't weigh them down either.

Campfire Girls was different, a weekly escape that shaped me in ways I didn't expect. Every meeting was a chance to gather with friends, to work on projects that gave structure to my restless energy. We followed patterns to earn awards, each task a small puzzle to solve, from crafting to community service. I put myself into them always relishing the sense of accomplishment when I complete a set of chores for a badge.

In time, I earned the National Torchbearer in Social Leadership Award; the highest honor in Campfire Girls and the pride of that moment still lingers. Those hours were a rare peace with my mother, a time when we didn't clash. We'd sit together, comfortable, no fussing or tension just a shared purpose. Campfire Girls was a haven, a place where I felt secure, where I could forget whatever was bothering me and focus on creating something with others.

We had award ceremonies and meetings, steady routines I could count on. I loved reliability, knowing I had to be with the friends I cared for; working side by side. I'd watch the flames bopping and their glow was warm against the night and feel a deep calm relaxation over me.

Even now, a fire sparks thoughts of vast things, like what lies beyond the universe, questions I never pondered as a child. Back then, it was enough to feel free, to let the fire's rhythm ease my mind.

By then, I already knew the sting of being dismissed in my father's science club, but I kept it going. He set them up with high hopes, gathering neighborhood boys to experiment in our home lab. We learned to measure things, pouring liquids into beakers or lining up rulers to mark lengths, the air sharp with the aroma of chemicals.

But the boys didn't care for science. They'd chase me out, saying girls couldn't do it, their taunts echoing in the room. The club fizzled after a few weeks, the experiments too basic and the tension too high. I barely recall the details, maybe because the rejection stung more than the lessons stuck. Still, those moments planted a seed, a quiet solution came to prove them wrong.

My love for science was crystallized in high school, despite the early setbacks. I started my own experiments, driven by a curiosity that led me to the National Science Fair. By my senior year, my father and I watched a television program on physics, the *Continental Classroom*, its lessons sparking a thrill in me.

I'd sit in the predawn quiet, the screen's glow lighting the room and think this is worth learning. That was when I knew I had to be a scientist, not because of the science club. The pursuit of knowledge felt like home, a place where I belonged.

Music and science didn't blend so much as co-existence in my life. I loved science for its puzzles, the way it let me dig into problems like air pollution at an aluminum forge plant. It was plants and it was me. Music was different, a release. I'd sing in choirs, the soprano, alto, tenor and bass blending into a chord that felt alive, like being part of something bigger.

I enjoyed the harmony, the way my voice joined others to create something whole. Once, at Dartmouth, I tried opera workshop, wondering if I could be a professional singer. But while waiting to perform, I found myself reading a science magazine, the pages pulling me back to my true profession. Singing was relaxing, a way to oxygenate my brain before diving back into science. I understood the music's frequencies and science behind the notes, but my love in science increases.

My peers didn't always notice my ambitions. In grade school, I helped a girl learn to read and quietly act of kindness occurs, but most didn't comment on my drive. In high school, I had a boyfriend who shared my love for science and math. We'd talk for hours, our minds sparking off each other, until he went to Caltech, where women weren't admitted then.

Years later, I saw his name on a national floodplain report and tracked him down, flying out for dinner, the memory of our connection as vivid as ever. That rediscovery felt like a gift, a reminder of shared dreams.

Mentors in college and graduate school cheered me on and never making me feel out of place in science's male-dominated world. Their encouragement was quiet. A nod to my ability that kept me moving forward. In group settings, whether it was singing in a choir or solving a science problem. I felt joy and belonging. Choral singing was a living thing, each voice weaving into a whole. Science was personal, a direct line to my core, where solving a problem felt as natural as breathing.

Those early influences, especially my father's push for science and shaped my lifelong pursuit of knowledge. His lab, his magazines and even the failed science club steeped me in a world of investigation. Building air conditioners at his store, watching water run through nets, sparked questions about how things worked. Science wasn't just a subject; it was my way of seeing the world. A lens for solving problems and finding truth. From the firelight of Campfire Girls to the quiet of my experiments, I learned to keep at it and to chase what mattered and to find joy in the pursuit.

Chapter 6

First Love & New Directions

In the waning years of my life; heart found its first spark of love; a brilliant high school boyfriend whose mind matched with me. Alongside that romance, I carved out spaces for solitude and discovery, from the quiet of my backyard study to the harmony of a church choir. Those years were a turning point, where I began to own my path, blending the thrill of connection with the steady pursuit of knowledge.

My love for science, especially quantum physics, deepened and though love and distance pulled me in new directions, I learned to trust my own ambitions, building a quiet life of intellectual depth that would guide me forward.

My high school boyfriend was a mathematician who was sharp and certain. The person who always knew the answer in class. We met in school, seated one in front of the other, our conversations spilled over into shared dreams and ideas. My mother had pushed another boy, the son of her best friend, but that connection faded quickly.

The boy from my high school was brilliant, his mind had a whirl of numbers and logic that I admired, especially since I was no slouch in math myself. During the summer after our senior year, he came to my house nearly every night and the warm Kansas evenings filled with our discussions.

We'd sit close, the air heavy with the promise of our futures he talked about Caltech and my opinion was Wellesley. Those nights felt like we understood each other completely, two minds in sync, sharing a familiarity that made the world feel bigger and brighter.

The dream of Caltech wasn't mine, not really. I wanted to be there only to stay near him, not because I thought it was better than Wellesley. His brilliance didn't reshape my ambitions; it just made me ache at the thought of parting. When summer ended, we had no choice but to separate, our paths diverging across the country. The disappointment stung, a quiet sadness for what we'd lost, but I didn't let it disrupt me. I wrote to him sometimes, trading thoughts on math, but I turned inward, focusing on my own work, becoming myself again without him.

First love taught me something subtle about myself, though it's hard to pin down. It wasn't a grand lesson. It was just a feeling, a heart-knowing that I could connect deeply with someone who saw the world as I did. Those summer nights, filled with laughter and shared ideas which showed me I could be seen, understood and valued for my mind.

That closeness carried me through the solitude that followed, a reminder that I was enough on my own. Privacy was my ally that summer and I found joy in it. By days, I worked in a hospital laboratory, running experiments in a quiet space that felt like my own. The hum of equipment and the sharp smell of chemicals became my world. A place where I could lose myself completely in science.

I was researching and solving the puzzles that no one else dictated. Working in those hours alone, focused on my work, was a kind of freedom. A chance to explore my thoughts without interruption. They balanced the warmth of my boyfriend's visits, grounding me in my own drive.

Music played a quieter role for me and a soft thread in my life. I sang in the church choir the year before that summer and maybe a little during it. Singing wasn't a passion, but it gave me a sense of belonging, like being part of something larger.

When I sang, my voice blended with others weaving into a chord that felt whole, grand, alive. It was like my time with my boyfriend, that same feeling of connection, of being part of something real. Music didn't drive me like science did, but it was comfort, a way to feel whole when I wasn't solving equations or running experiments.

It was in that little backyard playhouse which my parents had relocated behind my bedroom that my intellectual life began to grow. It was not only that summer but it was something that lasted throughout high school. I used to sneak out there in the early mornings before the world got up and do my science fair projects or read about quantum physics.

It was my own space, a peaceful place that I could be with my thoughts. It was cool; the table was littered with papers and materials and in that silence. I was free to experiment with ideas, to pursue questions concerning light and matter. It was not about a place to grow, it was about a place to be myself, to think without having the expectations of others.

The internal drive started to take a break with the outside force when I was in high school, particularly when I immersed myself in science fairs. I would come up with a thought, such as researching mold or the surface tension of water and how to make it occur all by myself. I would collect materials, construct apparatus and conduct experiments in my playhouse, and do them in the predawn silence.

Those projects brought me to the local and national science fairs where I received prizes. Not because I was driven to do it by anybody but because I chose to do it. It was then that I began to possess my own way, believing in my own interest in guiding me.

The field I liked the most was quantum physics. The play of light with matter and the weird dance of particles always seemed to me a puzzle to which I was born to find the answer. To this day, I am attracted to the questions of the origin of life, the areas of our union, such as human conversation as a type of energy.

I have questioned God, as well, but not in the sense of a rule-maker, but in the sense of a spur of the creation of the world. Those questions started in high school, fueled by my boyfriend's brilliance and my own growing confidence. Watching *Continental Classroom* with my father, the physics lessons flickering on the screen, I knew in future science was my profession.

Love, music and academics never felt at odds. I wove them together, choosing relationships with people who shared my interests, like my boyfriend. We'd talk about math or science; our conversations became a bridge between heart and mind. If I needed to study, I'd say so, carving out hours to read before meeting him.

It was natural, balancing connection with my pursuit of knowledge, never letting one overshadow the other. That summer was when I truly began to own my path. My boyfriend helped me see myself, not just as his partner but as a scientist and a thinker.

His presence and his wisdom gave me permission to embrace my own. The disappointment of our parting, when he went to Caltech and I to Wellesley, didn't break me. It redirected me, pushing me to focus on my own work. Years later, I saw his name on a national floodplain report and the thrill of that discovery sent me rapidly to meet him for dinner, a reminder of the spark we'd shared.

The intellectual depth I built in those years was quiet but fierce. My boyfriend's smartness in math, our conversations about science, helped me dig into the real questions of physics. I didn't need to be anything other than a scientist and that was enough. In my study space, in the hospital lab and in the choir's harmony, I found a life of purpose, one I shaped with my own hands and ready for the new directions that lay ahead.

Chapter 7

Ivy League and Independence

When I left Kansas for Wellesley, I carried with me a combination of obedience and curiosity. My father had pushed me toward physics for years, because he has unfulfilled dream of being a scientist and could find his life in me. I followed his urging and declared that path, though my own understanding of what it meant to live as a scientist and it was still forming. Physics had fascinated me in high school, but fascination was not yet the same as vision. At the beginning, I simply walked the road he laid out for me.

Wellesley was a place of freedom. For women, there was no boundary set on what subjects we might pursue. In every classroom, women filled the seats, ready to learn whatever was offered. I did not feel set apart or diminished because of my gender. At Wellesley, we were just students. The importance of study was expected and the environment gave me space to find my worth without the constant reminder that women were supposed to stay in other fields.

My courses kept me busy, but they did not isolate me. My life was full of friends, conversations and the steady routine of study. I began to see myself not only as my father's daughter who was fulfilling his hopes. I also find myself as a woman who was learning to stand on her own. The hours in classrooms and laboratories shaped me into a person who could meet challenges with quiet strength. There were no warnings at Wellesley that women should stay out of science. Instead, there was trust that if you wished to learn then you could.

Harvard University was a different place, though not an obstacle some might imagine. I walked into its classrooms aware that I was now stepping into a world dominated by men.

Professors seemed surprised at times that I had chosen their advanced courses, but I was not barred from taking them. I did not recall being treated as less capable, though I knew I had to prove myself in every test and every assignment. Not because I was a woman just because all students had to prove themselves. I worked hard, as hard as anyone, determined that no one could say I had not earned my place.

There it was natural to competition. Each of the students wanted to be the best and to be at the top of the class. I did not compare myself with men but the demands of the object itself. Physics and chemistry did not enquire whether you are a male or a female. They questioned whether you were able to understand the problems, solve them and gave you the strength to go on.

This was also the period when my life as a person started to change. I married a student from MIT. He was an engineer having his ambitions. We were just two youthful individuals who wanted to develop in the spheres of our interests. We did not have great evenings, but we had evenings. We would prepare meals together where the little apartment was filled with the aroma of dishes I was starting to gather. I became interested in cooking food and flipping through magazines and clipping recipes as he worked on his engineering problems. On weekends we mowed the lawn of our rented house in Cambridge small bits of regular life to keep us in the midst of our schoolwork.

Marriage and school were not initially a challenge. Both of us were in the youthful energy of crashing through courses and assignments thinking that we were capable of everything. My life became more complex when I got pregnant some years later and, still, continued working on my doctoral project. But still, I did not give up my studies at that time. Long days in the lab, frequently in the dark rooms with the sensitive experiments, I worked on my thesis. The desire to learn was not put to rest by marriage. Motherhood did not stop me. I kept moving forward.

Of course there were academic difficulties. It was a

mathematics course and one of the most difficult moments was during an advance. It was because I thought it would prepare me to do quantum mechanics. The task required some complex manipulations with matrices, long rows and columns of numbers which were to be solved manually.

To do them was to multiply diagonals and continue the process indefinitely, the kind of thing that would now be done in a little machine in a few seconds. However, then we did not have calculators. I found it difficult, more so when under timed exams. I failed one of them outright. The disappointment was keen, but the professor knew I had it hard. Patience enabled me to proceed, but I took away with me the lesson that brilliance was never sufficient in itself. Constancy, discipline and modesty were equally important.

The greatest challenge was later in graduate school. I was doing research in the area of vision, which deals with how light reacts with molecules in the eye. My tutor was a famous scientist. Through my stay there I was awarded the Nobel Prize. I was proud of being in his lab at first. He even requested me to be his photographer during the announcement of the award and I spent that day behind a camera to capture a moment that would have appeared to define the future of the field.

But success has its dark sides. As I did my own thesis work, I started to accumulate results that were mutely indicating conflict with certain of his conclusions. I never quite knew whether he felt it or heard it, or whether it was the other people who told him so. The only thing I knew was that he no longer talked to me in my final year in the lab. The silence was deafening. I kept on with my work, but with that absence I had to drag along.

I was conducting experiments on the subject of surface tension in water work, which was not part of my thesis, one day when I was doing so, when a postdoctoral researcher approached me and inquired why I had taken the time to do this work so far off course. I admitted that I was frozen, that I was not guided by my advisor anymore. He stared at me in a plain direction and told me,

I do not suppose that he will sign your thesis. Your findings discredit his reward.

What I was already starting to feel was confirmed by his words. If I stayed, I would not finish.

Leaving Harvard was not easy. It also implied a change of school to the University of Maryland and a new beginning in most respects. It was also the burden of silent sorrow of losing a child in those years. Such grief was compounded by the sterile hours in the labs which were full of liquid helium and the requirements of the experiments which left a small space to heal. But still I never stopped. I kept on teaching at a new university as I was continuing my research and raising my family.

Leaving was not a rebellion. It was survival. I was not devastated by external demands; I was not struggling with some huge fight against culture.

My father, once so insistent on physics, was far away and uninvolved. My husband supported me but did not demand that I follow his path. The pressure was my own, the weight of wanting to succeed and to remain true to my curiosity. When the path at Harvard closed, I found another. That choice became my declaration of independence.

There were no mentors guiding me through the transition. I had to navigate it on my own. Courage, in those days, did not feel like courage. It felt like necessity. One step after another, doing what needed to be done. I did not think of myself as resisting cultural expectations or proving that women could thrive in science. I simply did the work before me. I believed then and still believe, that the only real expectation worth following is the one you set for yourself.

Looking back, I can see the pattern. Wellesley gave me the

foundation. Harvard tested me. Marriage and motherhood gave me both joy and responsibility. The conflict with my advisor pushed me toward independence, forcing me to claim my own future instead of depending on the direction of others. Each challenge was not a wall but a turning, a shift in the path that carried me forward.

And to young women going into male spaces today, I would not advise them to struggle to show them that they can belong. I would tell them to work. Concentrate on work, be truthful, be tenacious. Do what you need to do best and do it. The world will catch up. You are not always going to have mentors. You will not necessarily receive the support that you need. But you may always make your own choice.

Freedom is not a decision. It is the custom of repeatedly making the decision not to switch directions. In my case, that implied dropping out of Harvard when I would have been silent by remaining. It was completing a degree at Maryland in case of others who could have dropped out. It was the changing of physics into air pollution when the questions of the world were pressing more upon me than the narrow task of molecules.

No moment occurred that could be called dramatic where I said this is my future. Rather, there was a gradual unraveling. One course at a time. One lab at a time. One job at a time. And the silent reminder that I was never enslaved to the dreams of my father, the silence of a counselor, or demands of anybody. I was not tied down, I could continue to build, I could continue to learn, I could continue to move. That was freedom, difficult to win, and silently defended, which made the core of my independence.

Chapter 8

Building Life Beyond
the Institution

My stay at Dartmouth was not terminated by a departure which I had arranged very thoughtfully. This occurred during a normal afternoon when the phone called in my office. There was a dean on the other side who was in the decline of his career. His language was short and conclusive. He told me that he was going to be replacing my graduate students and the research I had been undertaking and that my time at Dartmouth was over. The discussion took just minutes and it brought an end to years of work. I dropped the telephone and sensed an end of it all. There was no room for protest. The decision was made.

I went out of my office and drove over the river to my house and was still taking in the loss. On the table is the latest print of the science magazine. On the back pages there, as ever, were advertisements of positions in science around the country. I flipped through and found an announcement by Dartmouth Medical School. They were looking to find someone to revise a book to be used by the poison control centers.

I read it, got up and drove right back to campus. In a few hours after they had informed me that my post was finished, I had another. By afternoon, I received the offer to write and prepare updates to the poison control centers, which was a task that would fit perfectly in my life and I could continue taking care of my children and my career was not dead.

I had to juggle that work with family and complete the analysis of my doctoral thesis in four years. It was permanent, real and it did not have institutional politics looming upon it. But those years passed and I experienced the attraction to something new. I had been brought up in an environment of self-made businesspeople. I was shown by my father, my grandfather and friends of the family that I could be independent in work. Therefore, when the thought of entering the consulting space came about, it did not appear to be a stretch. It was as though it were a continuation of a tradition.

The initial call was by friends around Dartmouth who required assistance on local environmental problems. Shortly after that I put a two-line advertisement on science magazine, where I had previously discovered my place at the medical school. Soon a man called, almost immediately. He was a cement plant owner in Maine and he required assistance in securing an air permit. I accepted the job, went to the plant and soon realized that consulting was more than just a theoretical study. It needed practical solutions, keen observation and the capability to shift among technical knowledge and human issues.

The work grew quickly. The cement plant led to further projects and before long I was invited to consult for Martin Marietta Corporation in Baltimore. That opportunity changed the course of my career and my life. At Martin Marietta I met the man who would become my second husband. He was a physicist, skilled in measuring air pollutants at their source. My own strength lay in modeling, in using computers to trace how plumes moved once they left the stacks. Together we made a formidable team.

Our skills complemented one another and as we spent hours working side by side, we discovered not only professional respect but also personal connection. Within two years of joining Martin Marietta, I was promoted to Technical Director for Atmospheric Science, overseeing air pollution issues from twenty-five facilities across the country. The promotion also made me my future husband's boss. We decided the simplest solution was marriage.

Those early years of consulting were full of discovery. Each project opened a new set of questions. Unlike the steady curriculum of academia, consulting required me to learn at speed. Regulations shifted. Emissions varied from industry to industry. No two plants were the same. I read every issue of *Science*, scoured the Federal Register and attended meetings of the Air Pollution Control Association. At first I was just another participant, listening to experts present their findings. But soon I was asked to chair sessions, to write reports and to publish papers. I was no longer absorbing knowledge. I was shaping it.

My first independent project was not glamorous. It involved odors in the surgical suite of a local hospital. With a rented carbon monoxide monitor in hand, I walked the halls, tracing the migration of air. The source proved to be the trucks parked beneath the air intake in the early mornings. Their exhaust seeped upward into the operating rooms. Once that problem was solved, I traced other odors to taxis and buses idling at the hospital entrance.

Each solution came not from grand theory but from walking, watching and asking simple questions. The hardest discovery was that the neonatal care unit, where premature infants were treated, sat directly in the path of the Dartmouth power plant plume. The problem was stark and though no easy fix emerged, the experience marked me. I saw in concrete terms how emissions from one source could touch the most vulnerable lives.

From the hospital I moved on to a nearby tannery. The town was alive with complaints about odor and the tannery stretched over nearly two blocks. I began by inspecting where the sewage from the tannery joined the city lines. There I found a leak that was releasing foul smells into the neighborhood. Repairing it solved one problem, but soon residents on another side of the plant began to complain.

I handed notebooks to tenants in apartments across from the tannery and asked them to record when they smelled odors and which way the wind was blowing. Their notes led me directly to a six-inch pipe on the roof that was venting unchecked emissions. Fixing it quieted that side of the dispute. Then, in the spring, as snow melted, new complaints arose.

Trucks carrying raw hides dripped as they warmed in the sun, releasing smells that spread across the town. When I asked about the ground beneath the parking lot, I learned it was an old pile of coal. We had it removed and though residents complained about the stench of the coal as it was hauled away, the source of odor was gone. The tannery taught me that solutions often required patience, community involvement and persistence.

Martin Marietta opened the door to larger projects. I worked on emissions from steel mills and cement plants, learning the complex chemistry of their processes. I reviewed release forms for nuclear plants in Virginia and traveled across the country to aluminum reduction facilities in Washington State. Those plants were vast, their furnaces heating alumina to extreme temperatures and sending fumes into the surrounding air.

The work was challenging, but it also carried unexpected moments of beauty. I remember climbing a ladder bolted into the wall of a facility and reaching the top just in time to see a sunset spread across eastern Washington. It was a reminder that even in the midst of industry, the natural world remained present, worth protecting.

The challenges were rarely technical alone. Sometimes plant managers resisted the idea of reducing emissions. Sometimes the data was incomplete and I had to search through journals and reports, piecing together enough evidence to create a plan. Each project demanded both science and diplomacy. But each success strengthened my confidence that I was not only surviving outside the walls of institutions but thriving.

One of the more complex assignments came years later in St. Croix. A power company there needed an emissions permit for a new generator. The manufacturer claimed it operated at sixteen megawatts, but my own inspection suggested it performed closer to fourteen at sea level. The difference mattered. It changed the entire emissions profile. At first, officials at the Environmental Protection Agency refused to accept my calculations.

I pressed the case, pointing to the conditions I had documented. After months of back and forth, I proposed that the question be sent to the EPA's headquarters in Research Triangle Park. When the rule came back, it was in my favor. The permit was granted and the plant provided the power the island needed. That victory was not just technical. It was a moment when persistence and evidence overcame doubt.

Through all of these projects, I never felt limited by being a woman in the field. When I walked into plants, managers might raise an eyebrow, but once they saw the work, skepticism faded. I was judged by my solutions, not by my gender. The satisfaction came not only from solving problems but from seeing the relief on faces when a long-standing issue was finally addressed.

Building a business carried risks, but I did not dwell on them. Each project led to the next and each success brought new opportunities. With my husband beside me, both as partners and equals, we built a career that gave us not only stability but freedom. The ability to move where we wanted, the ability to decide on our projects, the ability to make our own life.

In retrospect, the abandonment of Dartmouth was more of a liberation than a departure. It pushed me out of the system of academia and into a broader environment in which the issues were urgent and the effect was tangible. I learned that I was not to be afraid of independence but was to accept it. It also provided me with self-confidence, identity and a sense of purpose that no institution could give me.

The best of all was easy. We were well off in terms of money and time to reap the benefits of our work. We traveled. We saw the world. And we took away with us the gratification that our efforts had left behind us places purer, air purer and societies healthier. Career was not all that independence was. It was about life.

Chapter 9

Partnership and Professional Love

I did not meet Ken in a social circle or somewhere he could have a date. This happened in one of the halls on the Martin Marietta premises minutes after I had been employed to work on their air pollution team. I had reached Baltimore through a long and winding path which started with my dismissal at Dartmouth. By the time I went into such an office, I was already getting used to the concept of living outside an institution. The company provided me with an office, I dropped my bag and as I entered the hall my eyes bumped into his eyes. There was a sort of familiarity in that look as though part of me already knew that this man would count.

Ken was a physicist but heavily trained in the measurement of the source of the pollutants. He already had a good reputation; his intellect was keen and his presence was stable. I was struck at once by his clarity. He appeared brilliant yet at the same time approachable. An unusual equilibrium in a profession that tended to draw individuals who were neither.

I personally was interested in modeling and computer use to track the movement of emissions after they were emitted off a stack. My work and his work are like puzzles. His skill alone at first impressed me. Respect came naturally. Eventually that respect grew to love.

As I started out, we were all colleagues in the same projects in the corporation. For two years we had the opportunity to travel, to write reports, to hold conferences and to learn how to work together. He was calculating, tolerant and accurate. I was quick at creating models, extrapolating the trends in the data and estimating the behavior of the plumes when they got into the atmosphere. The work required both sides. He would measure, I would be a model and we would be able to provide clients with a complete picture.

Our friendship was not based on candlelight dinners or on any informal dates but on common work. We were creating trust projects project by project, report by report and discussion by discussion.

When I got the promotion to Technical Director in the Atmospheric Science department, I was put in charge of over twenty professionals, Ken included. That change led our relationship to be transparent to all. It was no longer possible to assume that we were merely workmates. Marriage was the best alternative that we settled on. He respected my leadership; I respected his experience and we both respected the strength of what we could accomplish. Marriage did not mean that one escaped work; rather it was a continuation of work.

We were partners based on mutual respect. Ken was a mathematical fighter and I was amazed by how he approached mathematical disputes. I believed his figures. And in exchange I had believed his computer models and his intuition of the movement of air over landscapes. When we had a permit application, one of us would describe emissions, either by literature or by direct measurement and the other superimposed their effect on surrounding communities.

Ken was able to establish experiments in the field to verify what I had projected. We were able to fill in one another without being egoistic or competitive. It never concerned who was right. It was the question of getting the problem solved.

In St. Croix, one of our first combined endeavors was done. Martin Marietta required new construction permits at an aluminum plant. Our skills were needed in the work. I was the modeler; he was the measurer and we both persuaded regulators that our solution was complete. It was also one of our first occasions to travel together, to experience what it is like, to bring our professional partnership to new locations. We soon found out that we not only liked the work, but the adventure of riding together.

Other times we had shared moments of professional collaboration and had bonded on a personal level. In Puerto Rico, at one point, a number of consulting firms were under contract to a big refinery. At the same meeting, Martin Marietta requested all of us to report on progress. Other companies hurried to the scene in order to work using company computers. I sent Ken on, because his long associations at the plant would afford him access to areas others might not be able to access.

I remained to complete documentation with the rest of our team and then caught up with him. During the meeting Ken outlined three obvious steps in the next stage. His swagger and authority made the competition to be quiet. Since then, we have been the only consultants to the company. I was even more impressed by seeing him win that contest with just a few words.

We juggled our careers without difficulty. We did not have conflicts when dividing tasks when a project came in. One of us would say, you take this part. I answered the other. Then we would shake hands and proceed on. It was no horse-pulling of credit, no fighting. He was the physicist, I was the modeler and we were a team. We both had confidence in each other in terms of intelligence and instincts. We knew that we were stronger together as opposed to being apart and this bonded us.

Work was not the problem, but the difficulties which arose were not between us. Permits were complicated. Industrial managers were opposed to changes. Regulators demanded detail. But Ken was cool as he went through it all. He encouraged me in case I was discouraged. Had he been roadblocked I intervened. We were in a state of continual, uninterrupted and actual support of each other. He was not only my husband. He was my co-pilot as it was.

Travel was made one of the delights of our life together. Work took us to all parts of the United States, to Puerto Rico, to St. Croix and farther. Still, we found time to make trips which had nothing to do with consulting. We visited Thailand and Nepal together; there we were taken riding on the elephants through the forest, rafting rivers, singing around fires with villagers who sang to us.

In Nepal, we were stuck in Nepal when our plane was late due to storms and townspeople crowded the small airport and waited until the hail stopped. As soon as the skies cleared we flew into the elephant camp, where days were spent in rides, hikes and the sight, never to be forgotten, of the elephants bathing happily in the river.

We skied in Austria, hiked in Scotland and made a day trip into Poland in Europe. In Canada we went back and back to Jasper and each year we walked the same paths and it felt comfortable knowing the mountains. We had to explore new landscapes in South America and discovered not only the surroundings but also ourselves as partners. Every journey had its own share of problems weather, languages and unknown roads but every problem just made us stronger and stronger to the idea that we could manage anything together.

Travel is not vacation. It was a continuation of our collaboration. The same habits that were able to get us through projects were able to get us through airports, border crossings and long hikes. I would solve a problem when he was unable to do so. If I could not, he would. We had absolute mutual trust. We were at home in any unfamiliar location since we were together.

Science and romance were frequently confused. Next time we will be talking about emissions statistics an hour later and arrange to hike on the weekend. Even minor domestic problems were set up in common. I recall the way we used our scientific reasoning in taking care of our swimming pool, how we thought over how we could keep it warm and clean all through the year.

It would have looked to others trivial. It was another piece of evidence to us that intellect and love were not distinct powers in our lives but that they were mixed.

I was as much molded professionally as personally by Ken. His assurance cheered me when I got my doubts. As chances presented themselves he encouraged me on. This constant presence helped me to be confident to risky, to increase our consulting activities and to believe in my own knowledge. His love at the same time provided me with a feeling of security that enabled me to be entirely myself. I did not have to struggle to control as well as to protect against criticism. I might be and he might be and we prospered.

In retrospect, the best part of our journey is not a particular project or a particular trip. Support is the same. He was affectionate, admiring and benevolent. He never ceased seeking means to make life easier, richer and happier. I felt nurtured, honored and so very close to my heart when I was standing in a refinery in Puerto Rico, when I was hiking in the Canadian Rockies and when I was sitting in my home office splitting up a new project. He made me think that it might be more than romance and more than professional cooperation in partnership. It was all with him and it was complete.

We created our life with the help of intelligence and affection, science and journeys, with faith and mutual labor. He was my consulting partner as well. He was my partner in living. Up to the very last moment I never questioned the possibility that the encounter of our eyes in that corridor had been the beginning of something unique. I had my equal in Ken and I had my companion. And we created our own world.

Chapter 10

Nurturing Music and Education

Laboratories, classrooms and business meetings not only characterized the course of my life. It was also considered by the buzzing of a child voice; the sound of a piano being practiced in a closed door and the constant inquiries of the young minds trying to make meaning of the world. Rearing kids and being in a high-demand job was one of the most characteristic issues of my life. I also got to know more about myself, my decisions and my values than I had ever imagined in that balance.

As a mother, the initiation of my path started in the years when I was still completing my PHD and lecturing at Federal City College in Washington, D.C. I was a married woman then and had a first husband. He was stable, encouraging and equally committed to his teaching career too. We were with the group of educators who assisted in the formation of the Federal City College, which is a new and crucial institution to students in the District of Columbia.

The establishment of such school was an innovative move. We had faith in providing students with opportunities, and particularly those students who had not had numerous opportunities previously. That vision was shared by my husband and our domestic life was closely connected with the beat of teaching, planning and constructing an academic community.

It is also the years of birth of our children. I had the burdens of graduate research, lectures and administrative tasks and I was learning to be a mom. In northern D.C. we had a small residence near a park where the children could play. Books, lesson plans and musical notes, were all in that house.

It was also full of fatigue, as neither my husband nor I had time

to spend much at the end of every day. We relied on reliable/
childcare. We invited a babysitter to live in our place and soon
he became part of our family. She had stability because she was
there when both of us were away long enough. Her presence
enabled us to continue working and provided our children with
someone to be with whom they worked and was always available
whenever we had less time to attend to our children.

In retrospect, I see how weak that balance was. My first
husband was a hard worker at Federal City and I was already
starting to stretch toward new heights that would later send
me away. However, in those years our family life was based on
education, discipline and the assumption that knowledge was the
surest path. It was my belief that I wanted to be the legacy of
my children.

When my academic path led me away from D.C. to Dartmouth
College, my husband and I had to adapt. By then, the children
were older and entering school. I carried them with me into this
new phase and once again, childcare became a central part of the
story. In Hanover, New Hampshire, I found that the school itself
offered before and after school care. That simple arrangement
brought peace of mind.

I even bought a house located on school grounds so that the
children could walk to their classes and then return safely. My
schedule as a professor of physical chemistry was relentless, yet
I never lost sight of their needs. Each decision about where to
live, where to work and how to structure our days was shaped by
the desire to give them security and consistency.

During these years, music became a thread that tied us together.
My own love for singing had never left me. I studied opera, sang
in choirs and sought out lessons even when my professional life
seemed overwhelming. Music was a way to stay whole. It was also
a way to connect with my children.

They grew up hearing rehearsals in the living room, seeing

me prepare for performances and eventually bringing their own instruments to family gatherings. My daughter took to the flute with discipline and grace. My son discovered joy in the guitar and soon our home was filled with the clashing sounds of teenage bands practicing late into the night.

Those moments were not always peaceful, but they were alive. They taught the children that discipline and creativity could exist together. They saw me study notes on a score just as carefully as I studied notes from a scientific report. They came to understand that effort, patience and repetition lead to mastery, whether in science or in music.

Life after Dartmouth carried me back to Maryland, this time to new research and eventually to my work with Martin Marietta. This stage brought difficult choices. My marriage to my first husband did not last. He remained deeply connected to our son, who became the apple of his grandfather's eye. I respected that bond and allowed my son to stay with his father and grandfather.

It was not an easy decision, but it was the one that kept peace in the family. My daughter, on the other hand, came with me. In Maryland, she thrived with the help of caring teachers, before-and-after school programs and neighbors who became extended family. At times I gave trusted caregivers a key to my house so that my daughter would have what she needed even if I was delayed by work.

The arrangement required trust, sacrifice and constant planning. I often took trains back and forth on weekends so that my children could spend time with both parents. There were seasons when it felt as if my suitcase was never fully unpacked. Still, the children adapted. They grew in resilience and in their own sense of independence.

Music again becomes the connection between us like a companion especially during family milestones. When I married my second husband music was only in his heart.

Music was again the medium that united us particularly in family events. When I got married to Ken, who is my second husband, music was central to the marriage. I sang, he sang and our children were standing proudly with their instruments. They played guitar and flute at the altar and we all raised our voices. It was not just a wedding. It was a statement that the family was strengthened through common utterance. The day is one of the clearest memories of our unity.

Promoting the music among the children was not a goal of making professional performers. It was instilling in them confidence, discipline and joy. I would have them realize that education was not limited to books and that creativity would get as much attention as logic. The fact is that I can sometimes suspect that I have not done enough. My profession dragged me in so many ways that nights of studying or hours of music coaching's were not common. Nevertheless, I never missed their open performances and I never undermined their achievements. I thought that the example of my own persistence in the laboratory or on a stage. It was a kind of counsel.

In retrospect, the years when I had my first husband in Federal City College formed a basis. Those years taught me that it was the same qualities that were needed in building institutions and in building families: vision, sacrifice and collaboration. They also showed me that not everything makes the partnerships last, even in the cases when both individuals are committed and hard-working ones. The children but went on with the lessons of those years. They were brought up in families where learning was valued, where music was respected and where inquisitiveness was never disapproved.

There was no painless work on the issue of balancing career and children. Missing dinners, rushing on trains and feeling like distance was too much were some of the missed moments. But within that struggle resilience was created. My children also learned that adults could meet expectations and still put love at the heart of things. They even watched me fall, but they also watched me come back and back to the business of taking care of them and of developing myself.

Nowadays, I do not just imagine nurturing music and education, but I imagine all the notes we sang or lessons we studied. I envision the decisions that must be made when one is tired, the ingenious methods of locating childcare, the trade-offs and the perseverance. I remember how the love of learning which had been passed not in lecture, but in life.

And I recollect the first husband whose silent power in my first years as a mother enabled me to think it was possible at all. His role in this narrative cannot be overlooked, since, without those introductions at Federal City College, the subsequent arc of my career as a scientist, teacher and mother may never have occurred in the way that it did.

In the end, nurturing music and education was about more than raising children. It was about nurturing myself, nurturing partnerships and nurturing the belief that creativity and knowledge together can carry us through even the most demanding seasons of life.

Chapter 11

Redefining Belief and Purpose

From an early age I felt the tug of belief. At Wellesley every student was required to take a course in Bible study. I remember sitting with the text open, fascinated by the stories and the way generations had shaped them. That course planted an unexpected thought in me: perhaps I would become a minister.

Three different times in my life I tried to follow that path. Each attempt was sincere, but each was turned aside once by circumstance, once by family and once by the weight of my own doubts. Still, the desire never left completely. There has always been reverence about the sacred that I have had, although my definition of sacred has been in a state of flux.

Science had now taken control of my mind as I matured. At Harvard and afterwards at Maryland I studied chemistry and physics. The deeper I learned about atomic structure and quantum theory, the more I had the sense that the roots of conventional religion were sliding under my feet. Electrons, protons and energy waves spoke of a universe much more complex than the verses in the bible that I had cherished. At Wellesley they had also taught us how much of the early Bible had been rewritten in the third century, reshaped by human hands. That recognition left me with a question: *if the record of divine truth was altered, what could be trusted as absolute?*

Yet I never abandoned faith. I continued to sing in church choirs everywhere I lived. I found community in the rhythm of hymns, in the quiet of a sanctuary, in the minister's call to live with compassion. Jesus, I decided, was a brilliant man with ideas the world still needs. I believe in his vision of kindness and service, but I could no longer bind myself to doctrines that contradicted the reality science unveiled. So, I built my own philosophy, one foot in the sanctuary and the other in the laboratory.

That balance came alive during my years in Vermont. The tiny Methodist church near our home had only thirteen members when I arrived. I offered to sing during the service and soon began drawing neighbors who had never bothered to come before. I was a good listener in the hymns, selecting what I could discern as voices of promise. So, I took those singers and made them a choir. In two years, the number had swelled to over a hundred.

The church eventually summoned a new minister whom I had suggested and a hundred and fifty people now crowded the pews. That experience entrenched in me something that I had always felt, which is that belief is not merely a doctrine. It is belief that occurs as individuals gather, raise their voices and generate meaning together.

Music and worship sustained one part of me, and science the other. Sociology, biology and human behavior as well as chemistry were introduced to me in graduate school at Johns Hopkins. I began to see that science was not only a set of equations and experiments it was a tool to improve lives. Later, as I built my consulting business, I used that tool daily.

When I advised a cement plant to limit its emissions or testified about air quality after a tire fire in California, I was practicing a form of ethics. My job was to protect the public. The people who lived near smokestacks or who breathed the ash from an industrial accident deserved to be safe. To me that was not only professional responsibility but also moral purpose.

I recall one town in New Jersey that planned to compost household waste and spread it on farmland. My research revealed that toxic metals would accumulate in the soil. I argued that building a waste incinerator with proper controls would be safer. At a town meeting filled with several hundred people I presented the case. They voted overwhelmingly in favor of the incinerator.

In the end the town leaders rejected the project, but I felt I had done my duty. I used reason, evidence and ethics to try to guide a community toward health.

Reason was always my compass. My parents taught me as a child to think for myself, to solve problems, to examine facts before choosing. That habit carried into every corner of my life. Whether I was modeling air currents from an aluminum plant or making a decision about moving my family, I approached it by weighing evidence, considering consequences and planning ahead. I was rarely impulsive.

Planning became my way of survival. When one dean at Dartmouth ended my research program with a single phone call, I immediately searched the back pages of science magazine for new opportunities. Within hours I found a new position writing updates for medical reference books used in poison control centers. That small act of planning ahead set in motion the chain of events that eventually introduced me to Ken and to the career that defined my life.

Travel also widened my perspective. In Thailand, Nepal, Europe and South America I encountered diverse cultures and faiths. I saw temples filled with incense, cathedrals echoing with centuries of prayer, villages where traditions blended into daily labor. These experiences deepened my conviction that no single religion holds the whole truth. Humanity's wisdom is scattered, each community carrying a piece. What matters is not which piece being correct but whether we can live together without war, whether we can use our collective knowledge to reduce suffering.

The Unitarian church has become my home because it welcomes that diversity. There, no one demands strict adherence to creed. Instead, we gather around shared values: justice, compassion, respect for the interdependent web of life. That, to me, is religion at its best and opens doors to human progress.

Always learning has been the thread that holds my life together.

Science changes with astonishing speed. When I first studied physics, atoms were simple: nuclei with protons and neutrons, electrons orbiting in shells. Decades later I listened to an MIT lecture explaining that even neutrons and electrons are made of smaller particles, carrying charges in ways I had never imagined.

Reality itself was being redefined. Computers, too, reshaped my work constantly. Models grew more powerful. Data multiplied. I learned because I had no choice but without continuous learning the world would outpace me. And I learned because curiosity itself was a form of faith: faith that truth exists, faith that we can approach it more closely if we never stop asking questions.

Of course, learning was not limited to laboratories. Life itself requires flexibility. Uncertainty was constant whether I would find reliable childcare, whether a business contract would come through, whether a legal battle would be won or lost. In such moments I relied on the problem solver within me. I would study the uncertainty, list the options and search for the best path. That mindset gave me resilience. It taught my children resilience as well, showing them that obstacles can be met with creativity instead of despair.

Ethics guided the direction of that resilience. My simple rule was to provide support and safety for as many people as I could. That meant standing with communities fighting pollution, supporting global efforts to reduce emissions and insisting on honesty in professional testimony. Even in personal life I applied the same principle: help others live more comfortably, more securely, more freely. That, I believe, is what both science and religion point toward when stripped of complexity: the duty to nurture life.

I never saw reason and emotion as enemies. They flowed together, each tempering the other. Emotion gave me passion to fight for cleaner air or to build a choir from thirteen members into one hundred. Reason gave me the structure to make arguments clear, to model emissions accurately, to plan the next steps. If there were times I leaned too heavily on one side, I trusted the balance would return.

Looking back, I do not claim to have solved the riddle of belief. I remain convinced that there must be a God, though not in the simple image painted in Sunday school. The universe itself its order, its mystery demands an origin. Perhaps ours is one of ten thousand universes, but even so, the existence of creation points to a source. I choose to call that source God, though I do not imagine him as a figure with a beard in the sky. Instead, I see God as the great function of reality, the process that set energy and matter into motion.

If I were to offer advice to someone struggling between faith and reason, I would tell them this: you do not need to choose. Faith and reason are not enemies. They are companions, each pointing toward truth in different languages. Faith can give hope when reason falls silent. When faith is blind, reason can provide clarity. They can all assist us to adjust to the future. And change is sure to come.

Man is infinitely flexible. We can experience global warming, political upheaval or revolution in science that we are yet to imagine. But we will do it, as we always have. I have been contributing a little bit: teaching, singing, consulting, to write, to testify. Every move is made on the way ahead. I trust not in a creed but in the strength of learning, of thinking, of daily morals. That is my intention and it has seen me through all the trials.

In the end, redefining belief does not mean losing faith. It has meant expanding it. Faith in God as creator, faith in science as revealer, faith in humanity as builder of a better tomorrow. That faith, combined with reason, has been the compass of my life.

Chapter 12

Advice to Future Generations

When I think about the future, I do not imagine it as a straight line of certainty. Life has never unfolded that way for me, nor for anyone I have known. Yet I carry a deep and unshakable hope for the generations to come. Humanity, I am convinced, will always evolve to meet whatever challenges the Earth and society present. Even in times of hardship, I trust that we will survive, adapt and find a way forward. That belief more than anything else is the hope I leave for the future.

Trusting one's own mind has been an important lesson in my life, though it is not a simple command. Not every mind is trustworthy, at least not without reflection. To trust your mind, you must first examine it, test its reasoning and be sure you believe what it tells you. Only then is trust worthwhile. Blind trust can lead astray, but thoughtful trust can carry you through storms.

Taking risks has also shaped my path. One of the greatest risks I took was leaving Harvard and transferring to the University of Maryland, shifting from pure chemistry into atmospheric science. That choice altered the entire course of my career and ultimately opened doors that became my life's work. Risk is not always about danger; sometimes it is about allowing yourself to move in a new direction even when the outcome is uncertain.

I hope my story inspires curiosity. Reality is endlessly rich and there is great benefit in investigating it whether through science, through travel, or through the simple act of asking questions. To be curious is to be alive, to stretch beyond the immediate into the possible.

Courage, to me, is taking a step that feels both valuable and risky. It is not bravado but measured strength, cultivated by practicing on smaller risks until you know which ones are worth embracing. Courage grows like muscle. Each challenge prepared for you for the next.

If I am remembered at all, I hope it is as someone who helped pave the way for women to be strong in science. I was not the most famous scientist, nor did I solve every problem I faced, but I pressed forward and demonstrated that women belonged in laboratories, classrooms and conferences. I hope to be remembered as a scientist who tried, who contributed, who cared.

The legacy I want for my children and grandchildren is simple: if you keep at it, if you work with determination, you can achieve your goal. Persistence, not brilliance, is often the deciding factor in success.

Reason and love are sometimes spoken of as opposites, but I believe they can work together. My own balance was less about love versus reason than about action versus hesitation. Still, for future generations, I hope they learn to weave reason and compassion into one fabric thinking clearly while caring deeply.

Discipline plays a clear role in achieving dreams. Without discipline, goals remain wishes. With discipline, even difficult dreams come within reach. The same applies to creativity and responsibility. Young people can nurture both by remembering that human beings thrive when we care for one another. Creativity must serve others and responsibility must leave room for imagination.

If I were to give one guiding principle for life, it would be this: keep busy. Activity keeps the spirit alive. Busy can mean study, work, art, service, or simple curiosity it does not matter what form it takes, so long as you remain engaged.

As for my values, I hope they live on in this book. If there is any lesson here, it is that humanity matters. War, I believe, is an outdated inheritance from the animal world, a carryover of territorial instincts from wolves and whales. It is time for us to evolve beyond that. Human energy is better spent building, not destroying.

I have boxes filled with memories and stories, artifacts from decades of living. To me, they are reminders of who I was twenty, thirty, even fifty years ago. They connect me to earlier versions of myself and to the people and places that shaped me. They are untold stories still waiting to be revisited, treasures for anyone who cares to listen.

Challenges have been constant in my life, but I have learned that they are worth facing. You cannot avoid them all. Better to meet them head-on, evaluate them carefully and, if you believe you can overcome them, step forward with confidence.

If I could leave one final message for humanity, it would be this: **Humanity is a precious thing. Take care of it.**

That is the sum of all I have learned, distilled into one sentence. The world will change, science will advance, beliefs will shift, but the duty to cherish and protect one another remains. If future generations can carry that truth forward, then all my years of striving will have been worthwhile.